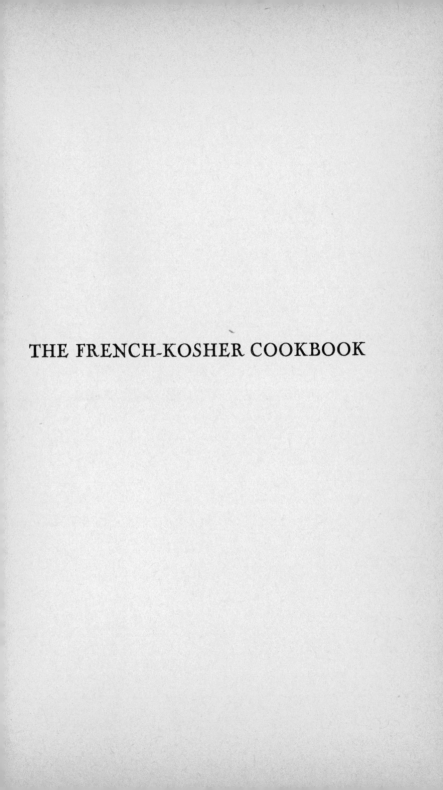

THE FRENCH-KOSHER COOKBOOK

THE FRENCH-KOSHER COOKBOOK

 BY RUTH AND BOB GROSSMAN

GALAHAD BOOKS · NEW YORK CITY

Published by Galahad Books, a division of A & W Promo-
tional Book Corporation, 95 Madison Avenue, New York,
N.Y. 10016, by arrangement with Paul S. Eriksson, Inc.,
119 West 57th Street, New York, N.Y. 10019.

Library of Congress Catalog Card No.: 73-81655
ISBN: 0-88365-086-X

Manufactured in the United States of America.

To Todd Adam—
the new kid on the block

All recipes in this book have been authenticated as Kosher by Rabbi Norman Siegel of the Jewish Center of Kings Highway, Brooklyn, New York

Thou shalt not eat any abominable thing . .

And every beast that parteth the hoof, and cleaveth the cleft into two claws, and chewest the cud among beasts, that ye shall eat . . .

These ye shall eat of all that are in the waters: all that have fins and scales shall ye eat . . .

Of all clean birds ye shall eat . . .

But these are they of which ye shall not eat: the eagle, the ossifrage and the osprey . . . and the glede, and the kite, and the vulture after his kind,

And every raven after his kind . . .

And every creeping thing that flieth is unclean unto you: they shall not be eaten . . .

But of all clean fowls ye may eat . . .

Ye shall not eat of any thing that dieth of itself . . . thou shalt not seethe a kid in his mother's milk . . .

DEUTERONOMY XIV

PREFACE

In most Kosher homes, there is a traditional culinary repertoire of dishes that are served with rather consistent regularity. And our homes were no exceptions. When Grandma, the *chef de cuisine* in Bob's home, found her grandchildren had become tired of the same limited dishes they had grown up with, she decided to do something about it to keep them coming over every week instead of wandering to greener, more delectable fields. So after coercing friends and family to assist her in gathering recipes of all nationalities, Grandma "took out from them the *hahzarye,*" and made them as tasty as the originals—but Kosher. We thought perhaps others would enjoy Grandma's recipes in her inimitable language and compiled them in THE CHINESE-KOSHER COOKBOOK, which was followed shortly thereafter by THE ITALIAN-KOSHER COOKBOOK. Having conquered these two cuisines, Grandma inevitably turned to what many consider the finest cuisine in the world—French cooking. But this really frightened her . . . for she heard the French used all sorts of cream sauces on meats! ate all kinds of non-Kosher shellfish and parts of animals she never even heard of! She had never really eaten true French food, but this was not going to deter her. Grandma felt a trip to France could give her all the background she would need to be able to take the *trafe* out of French food and make it Kosher, yet authentic. But Grandma is eighty three years old now and felt if she couldn't see all the gay spots of Paris and the museums and the famous landmarks—with maybe the Riviera thrown in—it really wouldn't be too much fun. And although she has lots of energy, Grandma had a better idea. She decided to send her grandchildren in her place . . . let us have all the fun, bring back the information, and then she could continue her seemingly endless job of making foods of all countries within the Dietary Laws. We had been to France before, but who could pass up such an offer! The reservations were made a year in advance so we could have a lovely ocean voyage aboard a truly French ship. New luggage was bought, a few new clothes purchased, spending money was saved . . . we read volumes of the latest tourist books on France . . . it was all we talked and thought about.

We never made that trip. And Grandma couldn't be happier. For now, in addition to our French poodle we have added a son, Todd Adam, to our family. And it looks like all our future recipes will have to read, "serves 4 or more." We never got to visit that synagogue in Lyon or the Hadassah group in Marseilles, but maybe next year . . .

Brooklyn Heights, N. Y.   Ruth & Bob Grossman

TABLE OF CONTENTS

THE FRENCH-KOSHER COOKBOOK

TRUFFLES SHMUFFLES!

From French food you can get heartburn, too. Like lots of other countries, France has its share of heavy food like BOEUF BOURGUIGNONE, which is really a beef stew with a fancy name. But nobody can make a nice delicate omelet or a CREPE SUZETTE (a fancy kind of blintz) like a Frenchman. Sometimes though, they surprise you with some of their *meshugenuh* food . . . calves' heads, frogs' legs, snails, woodcock with its own intestines yet, and even turtles. But in this book you'll find the kind of dishes you could bring home to Mother and she still wouldn't know what they were. But one thing sure—you'll know they're really French and they're guaranteed Kosher.

Before you start running to the stove, stop first and a little inventory you'll take in the kitchen. The French do most of their cooking in good heavy pots so the heat goes all over evenly, and it's pretty sure the foods won't stick and burn. Copper pots are nice to cook in and they look so *mench* sitting around a kitchen. . . . but if you don't have them, heavy enamel cast iron ones are wonderful. (Some of them are so heavy you could get a hernia, but such food you'll cook in them!) For your sauces you should have a big wire whisk. You could maybe live without one, but this looks very French in the kitchen. But what you can't live without is a good sieve so you can strain soups and sauces that need

1

straining, and they're good for puréeing vegetables and things. Your omelet pan shouldn't be just any pan you cook regular eggs in. It should be kept only for omelets. You never wash an omelet pan (the neighbors don't have to know . . . some things you should keep to yourself). You just wipe it clean with maybe a paper towel. This way it gets "seasoned" and your omelets never stick to it, because a stuck omelet becomes a scrambled egg.

All through this book you'll see, if you keep your eyes open, the words "bouquet garni". This has nothing to do with flowers. It's just a clean *shmatah* that holds lots of nice spices like sprigs of parsley, a little thyme, a bay leaf, peppercorns and sometimes a clove or two. You just tie a string around the bundle and let it sit in whatever you're cooking when the recipe says so and all those delicious flavors just cook in. Afterwards, you don't have to strain . . . just throw away the "bouquet garni".

You'll notice the French use a lot of wine in their cooking . . . but the alcohol cooks off, so don't worry about getting drunk. And when the recipe says a "dry" wine, don't use a sweet wine or everything will taste like dessert . . . there are plenty good Kosher dry wines.

Also, you'll see that some of these recipes call for different kinds cheeses. Again you shouldn't worry, there are plenty good Kosher cheeses.

Some people get shallots mixed up with scallions. But shallots are like a cross between onions and garlic and a scallion is a scallion. But if you can't get shallots, you can use the white parts of scallions. They're almost just as good.

Beurre manié is a wonderful way to make thick the juices in vegetables that some people throw out. To make it you knead together the same amount of butter and flour until it makes a soft ball. Then you break the ball into little pieces and drop it in the peas, beans or whatever you're binding together, and swirl it around until it's thickened. With a *fleishig* meal, you'll use *parve* oleo with the flour and it's just as good and a lot more Kosher.

Truffles are very popular in France and very expensive in America . . . so if you can afford to have truffles lying around the house, you'll throw away this book and hire your own French chef—but you'll make sure he's Kosher. Bon appétit!

2

HORS D'OEUVRES

PÂTÉ DE FOIE SCHMALTZ*

1 lb. chicken livers	¼ teaspoon white pepper
1 nice sliced onion	1 teaspoon salt
5 tablespoons schmaltz	¼ teaspoon savory
1 tablespoon sherry	

Broil first the livers. While they're broiling, you can fry in the schmaltz until golden and soft, the onion. Now add a little of the broiled livers and a little of the onion into the blender and blend. Blend a small batch at a time until it's all done. If you don't have a blender, chop up the whole works in a chopping bowl and then push it through a sieve. Now you can add the spices and the sherry, and mix yourself up good. Pour this into an ovenware bowl and cover it up tight. (If there's no cover, use foil.) Now stand this in a large pan with a few inches of water in it. Put the whole thing into a 400° oven and let it cook for 2 hours. Then you can chill and garnish with parsley and shredded carrots for a *forshpeis,* canape, or just plain *nosh.*

---

* *SCHMALTZ:* the Jewish answer to the 70¢ spread.

4

GEHAKTE PÂTÉ DE SACRE BLEU!*

1 lb. chicken livers
2 lbs. ground meat
1 onion, chopped
3 shallots, chopped
1 clove garlic, chopped
1 tablespoon chicken schmaltz
3 tablespoons solid Kosher vegetable shortening
2 nice eggs

½ cup dry red wine
1 tablespoon flour
½ teaspoon dry mustard
½ teaspoon white pepper
½ teaspoon ginger
1 teaspoon salt
1 tablespoon parsley
1 teaspoon MSG

First, broil the livers to "kosher" them. While you're broiling, you can sauté the onion, shallots and garlic in the schmaltz and shortening. When this is all done, mix it, schmaltz and all, together with the eggs, wine, flour and spices. Now you can purée this with the chicken livers in a blender, if you have. If you don't have, then chop up the livers nice and fine and mash them together with the other stuff. Now you'll mix up with the chopped meat and put the whole thing into a meat loaf pan and with foil you'll cover it. Put this pan into a bigger pan that has about an inch of water in it. Then the whole thing you can put into a 300° oven for 2 hours. For the last 20 minutes the foil you should take off. When it's all done, chill for at least 8 hours. After it's chilled, you'll dip the pan into hot water for 15 seconds. This will loosen it a little. Turn it upside down on a serving plate. If you dipped long enough it'll plop right out. Decorate the top a little with parsley or chopped hard-boiled egg . . . don't *umgepatch* too much. Now you'll slice it thin for a *forshpeis,* or if you're a real "big shot"—you'll have an hors d'oeuvre.

SACRE BLEU!: the French answer to *Oy Gevalt!*

5

KNISH LORRAINE*

FIRST, THE PASTRY SHELLS YOU'LL MAKE:

2 cups flour   ⅔ cup Kosher vegetable shortening
¾ teaspoon salt   7 tablespoons cold water

Sift good together the flour and the salt and then with 2 knives or with a pastry blender you'll cut in good the shortening until the pieces are like the size of grains of rice. Now, sprinkle on 1 tablespoon of water and mix it up with a fork. Then add the next tablespoon of water and mix, and you'll just keep doing this until all the water has been used and the dough is moist. Now take it out from the bowl in your hand, and press it together into a ball. (Don't be afraid. You can wash later your hands.) The ball you'll sit in the refrigerator for a few minutes. Then take it out and roll it on a floured table till it's a big sheet of dough about ⅛ inch thick. Cut the dough into 5 inch circles. For this you'll use a bowl or anything you've got lying around that's about that size. These circles of dough you'll mold nicely over an upside down muffin tin, and bake them in a 450° oven for 15 minutes. (Remember the muffin tin is upside down . . . it's no mistake.) When they're done, you'll take them off carefully from the muffin tins and all of a sudden, little cups you've got! Whatever you do, don't make any holes in the dough, or later everything will run out from the shells and will your face be red! This makes about 12 shells. If you're not exactly 12, that's all right too.

6

NOW, THE FILLING WE'LL MAKE:

1 thinly sliced onion	½ cup milk
2 teaspoons butter	½ teaspoon salt
4 lightly beaten eggs	A good pinch pepper
1 cup cream	½ cup diced Swiss cheese
¼ cup Parmesan cheese, grated	

First, you'll sauté the sliced onion in the butter until it's nice and soft. Meanwhile, together mix the eggs, cream, milk, salt and pepper. You'll put in each shell a few pieces of the sliced onion and on top of that put a little Swiss cheese. Now into each shell pour some of the egg-cream mixture. You'll put the same amount in each shell. On top of each, sprinkle the Parmesan cheese. Now very carefully put the shells on a cookie sheet or anything big and flat and put them in a 450° oven for about 25 minutes. Serve them right away, they're delicious hot. This, to tell you the truth, is not really a Knish; but then it's no Lorraine either. You try to put a filling like this in a real Knish and see what'll you'll get. Serves 12 delicate friends . . or 6 adventurers who like everything in two's.

*KNISH: a New York politician could never be elected without eating one.

AVOCADO VINAIGRETTE
GAY AVEC*

FOR THE VINAIGRETTE SAUCE, YOU'LL HAVE:

½ cup oil
¼ cup wine vinegar
A good pinch salt
An also good pinch black pepper

1 tablespoon chopped chives
1 tablespoon chopped parsley
2 nice size cloves garlic,
   chopped fine

½ teaspoon paprika

This is so simple to do, it's almost embarrassing. All you do is mix together everything, put it in a jar, and you'll give a nice shake.

NOW, THE MOST IMPORTANT THING OF ALL:

3 ripe avocados
A little shredded lettuce

With a sharp knife cut each avocado in half the long way around. Pull apart nice and easy, and take from the middle the big round pit. On each salad plate, you'll put some shredded lettuce, then a half of avocado, then you pour in the hole enough VINAIGRETTE SAUCE to almost fill the hole. If you should have any of the sauce left over, it makes a nice dressing for regular salads. This will serve 6 people who, believe me, had better like avocados or they'll just be out of luck.

*GAY AVEC: the new advertising slogan of Pierre Shapiro's Travel Bureau.

GEFILLTE FISH REMOULADE*

In France the Remoulade Sauce they make is like Tartar Sauce they make here. But in New Orleans, the French chefs make a Remoulade Sauce that's a Remoulade Sauce! This is how they do it:

2 tablespoons lemon juice	1 tablespoon parsley
2 tablespoons tarragon vinegar	A pinch black pepper
2 tablespoons prepared mustard	1 teaspoon paprika
2 tablespoons horseradish	A good sprinkle cayenne pepper
A good pinch salt	1 cup vegetable oil
	¼ cup fine chopped celery
	¼ cup fine chopped scallions

Mix together good the lemon juice, vinegar and the rest of the spices. Then throw in the oil, celery and scallions. This you'll blend together good with a beater, or even a blender.

FOR THE REST YOU'LL NEED:

1-1 lb. jar gefillte fish balls   Shredded lettuce, to serve on

Arrange nice the balls on some shredded lettuce and a little sauce you'll pour on. One thing you shouldn't forget, serve this good and cold. This should be enough for 4 or even 5 people. If you're not serving so many, you can put the rest of the sauce in the refrigerator for next time. It keeps for 120 years, it should live and be well.

*GEFILLTE FISH: a popular *forshpeis* in Catholic homes on Friday night.

9

FAHBISSENAH EGGS EN GELÉE*

FIRST, YOU'LL MAKE AN ASPIC WHICH, IF YOU DON'T LIKE, YOU'LL FORGET ABOUT THIS RECIPE:

1½ cups chicken broth
½ cup tomato juice
2 envelopes unflavored Kosher gelatin
½ teaspoon sugar

1 crushed eggshell
1 beaten egg white
Salt & pepper, it should taste
1 tablespoon cognac

Heat the chicken broth, tomato juice, gelatin, sugar, eggshells and whites, and salt and pepper all together. Pull up a chair, because you have to stir it constantly and you'll remove it from the heat when the whole thing boils up like a froth. Stir in the cognac (if you haven't finished it in the excitement) and then strain this mish-mash through a cloth, you'll make sure it's clean. Spoon about 3 tablespoons of the aspic into each of 4 custard cups you should have somewhere in the house. Put the cups in the refrigerator and leave them there until they get nice and firm.

NOW COMES THE REST OF IT:

4 eggs
4 thin slices of corned beef, about the size of the poached eggs

Poach the eggs and let them cool themselves on a plate. Take out from the refrigerator the custard cups and put in the cups a cooled egg in each one . . and on top of that you'll put a slice of the corned beef. Pour now the rest of the aspic divided nice and even into the custard cups and back into the refrigerator to chill. When it's time to unmold, and don't rush it (be sure it's nice and firm), dip each cup into a bowl of warm water and quick turn the cups upside down on individual serving plates. This *forshpeis* is so nice and delicate everybody will still have room for the rest of the meal and not get the cholesterol count pushed up too much. You can make it ahead of time so you'll be able to have a nice cocktail with your 3 guests, if you didn't sneak too much cognac from the aspic.

*FAHBISSENAH: if his smile was his umbrella, he'd get drenched!

10

SOUPS

L'OIGNON SOUP LEVINE
AND ROSE*

5 onions, thinly sliced
4 tablespoons oleo
7 cups vegetable bouillon
1 teaspoon sugar

1 cup dry white wine
Salt & pepper to taste
6 pieces crusty French bread
½ cup grated cheese

Sauté the onions in the oleo, they should be soft. Then you'll pour in the vegetable bouillon, the sugar and the wine and give a healthy stir. Put on the cover and you'll simmer for an hour. Then you'll put in the salt and pepper and taste it to see if it's enough. Don't overdo it; but on the other hand, onion soup has got to have a real taste. Put in each deep bowl one slice bread and over it you'll sprinkle with a lot of generosity the grated cheese. Pour the soup now over the bread in the bowl and eat hearty! This is a man-sized soup for 6 people or if you have dainty lady-size bowls, maybe you'll squeeze out a few more portions. Just be sure you have enough bread cut or you'll have hurt feelings, which don't mix well with onion soup.

*LEVINE AND ROSE: a French tune popular throughout the world.

QUEL DOMMAGE POTAGE DE PETITS POIS*

3½ cups shelled peas
½ cup heavy cream

1 teaspoon sugar
Salt & pepper to taste

Cook the peas in a half cup water with the sugar added, until they are nice and tender. Next you'll drain them and purée the peas with the cream in a blender, or a sieve if you never got around to buying that blender. Add enough salt and pepper so it should taste like something, and warm the soup . . . don't boil it or only you will be responsible . . . until it's comfortable enough to eat. This soup will have such a beautiful avocado color, you shouldn't know from it! And it will be very fattening for 4 skinny people. You can use canned peas for this dish—but somehow, that seems like cheating. But look—it's your business what you do in your kitchen. You do like your conscience says.

*QUEL DOMMAGE: when you write a check to the *shul* for a big donation and it bounces.

13

VEGETABLE SOUP SANS
PIÈCE DE RÉSISTANCE*

2 sliced onions	2 sliced carrots
2 stalks celery	A little salt, you should taste
2 tablespoons parve oleo	A couple dashes pepper
4 cups vegetable bouillon	A pinch marjoram
2 medium sliced potatoes	1 teaspoon MSG

2 tablespoons chopped parsley

Sauté nice the onions and celery in the oleo. In a pot you'll put the vegetable bouillon, the sautéed onions and celery, and also the raw potatoes and carrots. Cook this whole thing on a low fire until everything is soft. When this is done, purée everything through a sieve or put it in a blender until it's all nice and smooth. Put in now your seasonings—and don't be shy . . . nobody likes food that tastes like nothing. Simmer maybe 5 minutes more and you'll have a soup that'll bring smiles to 4 vegetarians.

* *PIÈCE DE RÉSISTANCE*: those little yellow eggs in the chicken soup Grandma gave you when you were good.

VICHYSSOISE DE MADAME POMPADOUR*

6 medium onions, sliced
5 medium potatoes,
   peeled & sliced thin
6 cups vegetable bouillon
3 cups milk

1 cup cream
1 teaspoon salt
½ teaspoon white pepper
2 teaspoons Worcestershire Sauce
¼ cup chopped chives

Mix the sliced onions together with the potatoes and the vegetable bouillon and cook it over a low heat for 45 minutes so the flavors get mixed up all nice and delicious. When it's done, push the whole thing through a sieve, it should be very fine. Stir in now the milk, cream, salt, pepper and Worcestershire Sauce. On top, sprinkle the chives and when it's cooled down a bit, put it into the refrigerator and let it get good and cold. Even though this is a heavy soup, for warm weather it's wonderful because it's cold. This may look like an anemic borsht, but it's a healthy soup for 8 run-down people.

*MADAME POMPADOUR: the famous *shiksa* with the famous *shaytel*.

BORSHT À L'ENFANT
TERRIBLE*

8-10 medium beets	Salt & pepper, it should taste
6 cups water	2 tablespoons lemon juice
1½ cups dry red wine	2-3 tablespoons sugar
	2 eggs beaten up nice

Wash and peel the beets nice and carefully. Next you'll grate the beets, but be careful you shouldn't grate your fingers too and make from the soup a big mess. In a large pot you'll put now the grated beets together with the water and wine. Add the salt and pepper and taste to be sure everybody else will be able to taste, too. Let the whole thing simmer for a half hour. Add now the lemon juice and the sugar, give a stir, and give another taste to be sure the borsht will be "sweet and sour-y" enough.

Take the pot from the fire and let it cool uncovered. Stir in the beaten up nice eggs and the soup's finished. You can serve it hot or you can put in the refrigerator and let it get nice and cold. Don't forget to serve with it a big tablespoon of sour cream in each bowl. This will make enough for 6 to 8 people who only *thought* they'd had good borsht before.

*L'ENFANT TERRIBLE: the kid next door who taught all the boys on the block how to smoke.

SALADS & DRESSINGS

NAOMI'S NICOISE SALAD*

2 cups cooked French style
  string beans
2 cups cooked diced potatoes
10 rolled anchovies

Several thin strips pimiento
½ cup pitted black olives
1 cup VINAIGRETTE SAUCE,
  see p. 8

Mix together good the string beans and potatoes with
the VINAIGRETTE SAUCE. Make one big heaping mound of
this mixture on a serving plate. Now you'll decorate this
mound with the anchovies, pimiento strips and olives. Some
people even like hard-boiled egg slices and tomato wedges to
decorate with. This is also good, but not an absolute must. This
fancy salad serves 4 fancy people and is especially popular with
people who usually can't stand salads.

*NAOMI: that poor girl in the Bible whose mother-in-law Ruth
was always *shlepping* along after her.

FAH TUHMULD TONGUE SALAD*

½ lb. cooked tongue
3 tablespoons oil
1 tablespoon wine vinegar
1 tablespoon chopped onions

1 tablespoon chopped chives
2 tablespoons chopped parsley
A little salt & pepper
Some lettuce to serve on

Slice thin the tongue into little strips. Mix together the oil, vinegar, onions, chives, parsley, salt and pepper and pour this whole thing over the tongue strips. Put the mixture on a bed of lettuce and serve it to 3 or 4 people maybe with a cool lemonade. This makes a good salad, hors d'oeuvre, or a nice hot-weather lunch. Anyhow, it's a good way to use leftover tongue. You might have to buy sliced tongue at a delicatessen, because cooked leftover tongue you won't find at the butcher.

*FAH TUHMULD: what happened when Miriam told her folks she had the lead in the school Christmas play.

19

SHADKEN SALADE À
LA RUSSE*

1 cup of diced cooked potatoes	½ cup chopped celery
1 cup of diced cooked chicken, leftover is nice	½ cup chopped beets, cooked
	½ cup chopped apples
½ cup cooked green peas, drained	Salt & pepper, a few pinches
	2 hard-boiled eggs
	1 cup mayonnaise

You'll remember first, this is a cold salad, so all those things that have to be cooked can be leftovers or cooked earlier and then made cold in the refrigerator. Then you'll mix everything together (except the eggs) with the mayonnaise. (If you have the time, you shouldn't miss making the mayonnaise that's on p. 54.) Pile it up nice in a serving dish and with the slices of hard-boiled egg, you'll decorate. With this salad, you can be so creative and mix all kinds things together if you don't have all these ingredients. Not even a Russian would know the difference! This'll serve 6 to 8 people depending on how much *hahzarye* you threw into the salad.

*SHADKEN: she's lobbying to get Sadie Hawkin's Day made a national holiday.

GREEN SHMENDRICK SALAD
AVEC DRESSING FRANÇAISE*

FOR THE DRESSING, YOU'LL NEED:

1 teaspoon altogether of parsley, chives, chervil & tarragon
1 tablespoon vinegar

3 tablespoons oil
¼ teaspoon prepared mustard

Mix everything together so all the flavors blend and you'll have *some* dressing!

FOR THE SALAD, YOU'LL NEED:

Lettuce
Romaine
Chicory

Escarole
1 clove garlic

You can use any or maybe all of the greens listed here and you'll wash them very carefully—who knows what kind of nonsense they sprayed on them!—and dry them very carefully. The French put the leaves in a little basket and shake them dry (you can use a paper towel) because they say the water will make the dressing weak. So you don't take any chances, dry already.

Rub with the clove garlic, the salad bowl—a wooden one is nice—put in the mixed greens, pour in the dressing and mix together like a real chef so all the leaves, they'll be coated. In France, this is the salad that seems to be everybody's favorite to eat with a meal . . . 400,000 Frenchmen can't be wrong, especially if they're all Jewish.

GREEN SHMENDRICK: a popular radio character who had a Philippine houseboy named Mendel.

EGG
&
MATZOH DISHES

TROMBENIK OMELET
AUX TRUFFES*

2 tablespoons chopped truffles
3 tablespoons butter
6 nice fresh eggs

2 tablespoons milk
1 tablespoon brandy
Salt & pepper to taste

Truffles are very special and very popular in France. In America, you'll buy them in certain stores in little cans, they're not cheap. You'll cook them nice in the butter in your favorite omelet pan—it should be a large one (11 inches across) with not·very high sides. In the meantime, you can mix up the eggs with the milk, brandy, salt and pepper. Take out from the pan the truffles and mix them in with the egg mixture. Pour the whole thing back into the omelet pan and cook on a medium fire until it sets nice. While it's setting, with a fork you'll lift the egg very little from the pan here and there and tilt the pan slightly, so the liquid mixture can run underneath. Keep doing this all around the pan the whole time it's cooking. It's not so complicated as it sounds. When the omelet looks like it's done, it probably is. Slide it out from the pan onto a plate and fold it in half, you'll be careful and don't rush. Cut it into serving portions—you can probably feed 2 or 3 people with it. A slice or two of toast . . . some nice fresh coffee . . . and you've got a real *mench* breakfast.

*TROMBENIK: if he did half the things he claims he did, there'd be two of him!

EGGS BENEDICT SANS HAHZARYE*

8 nice fresh eggs
8 thin slices baloney
8 slices toast with crust removed,
    you should be fancy
Parve HAYMISHA HOLLANDAISE SAUCE, see p. 30

First, you'll poach nice the eggs in a little salted water. While you're poaching, trim each slice baloney so it should be the same size as each piece toast. Now put one slice of baloney on each slice toast. Drain the poached eggs and put one on each slice baloney-covered toast. On top this whole thing you'll spoon a little HOLLANDAISE SAUCE, and keep spooning until it's all used up. Some people like this sauce so much . . . when they're finished with the eggs, they might ask for extra toast to wipe up the sauce. Maybe it's not what Amy Vanderbilt would do, but good is good . . . they should live and be healthy! This serves 8 light eaters or 4 who can put it away nicely.

*HAHZARYE: that greasy pig stuff!

24

SCRAMBLED OEUFS GRAND'MÈRE*

2 slices white bread,
  cut in ¼ inch cubes
3 tablespoons butter
8 nice fresh eggs

2 tablespoons milk
A pinch salt
A pinch pepper

Fry the bread cubes in the butter until they're crisp and brown and very appetizing looking. Now beat the eggs—but you'll beat lightly—with the milk, salt and pepper. Pour this into a pan you should butter generously, and make a medium fire under the pan. Stir the eggs and keep stirring until they're smooth and creamy and then put in the fried bread cubes. Mix them in nice with the eggs and it's ready to serve 4 hungry grandmothers, they should live and be well!

* GRAND'MÈRE: a *bubba* who has wine and cheese by the Seine instead of tea and cake on the stoop.

MESHUGENUH MUMZER
MATZOH BREI MORNAY*

FIRST, YOU'LL MAKE THE BREI:

4 matzohs   A good pinch salt & pepper
4 nice fresh eggs

Soak first the matzohs in some water so they'll get soft. Then you'll drain and mix in with the eggs, salt and pepper. Into a greased baking dish you can put this mish-mash and cook it in a 325° oven for 30 minutes. It'll rise a little bit and be much prettier than if you fried the matzohs—and you probably eat too much fried food anyway.

NOW, YOU'LL MAKE THE MORNAY SAUCE:

2 tablespoons butter   2 tablespoons Gruyère cheese, grated
2 tablespoons flour   ¼ teaspoon salt
1 cup of milk   A little black pepper

Melt the butter first in a saucepan on a low fire, and then stir in the flour, it should be smooth. Don't go anywhere; just stand there and keep stirring a little. Now you'll pour in slowly the milk (you're still stirring until it gets thick) and let it cook about 2 minutes more. Add now the cheese, salt and pepper —mix in good and *schoen!* a MORNAY SAUCE you have. This is a classic French sauce and you can use it over eggs, vegetables, and fish. But I'll give a penny for every French housewife who's ever used it with *Matzoh Brei*. . . .

When the *Matzoh Brei* is ready, you'll take it from the oven and cut it in wedges like you cut a pie. Spoon on a little sauce on top and you have nice Sunday brunch for 4 to 5 people. It tastes delicious with hot QUELLE HEURE-EST IL CAFÉ AU LAIT, see page 80.

*MESHUGENUH MUMZER: Abdel Nasser's Jewish name.

SAUCES

SAUCE BÉCHAMEL DE
BRIGHTON BEACH*

2 tablespoons butter	A little pinch salt & pepper
1 tablespoon minced onion	1 cup hot milk
2 tablespoons flour	

Melt in a saucepan the butter and cook in it the onion until it's nice and soft. Then you'll throw in the flour, stir it a little and cook a minute or two more, but don't let it get brown. Now you'll add slowly salt and pepper and pour in slowly the milk, it shouldn't get lumpy. Keep stirring all the time. (With these French sauces, when they say stir, it means you'll forget everything else and stir.) Cook this on a low fire and stir constantly until it gets nice and thick. After that you sit down and take a breath and just give a stir now and then and you'll be sure that fire is nice and low. Let this sauce cook gently for about 20 minutes, strain out the onion, and serve the sauce on eggs, vegetables, and fish.

The nice thing about this sauce is that if you add a little grated cheese to it, you'll have a nice CHEESE SAUCE; if you add a little sweet cream to it, you'll have a CREAM SAUCE; when you add a touch of curry, it'll make a tasty CURRY SAUCE; some prepared mustard stirred in makes a MUSTARD SAUCE, etc. And it's right every time.

This, by the French, is one of their most important sauces. When you know how to make it, you'll be like a *mayvin* of sauces and you'll probably get all kinds invitations to cater Bar Mitzvahs and sweet sixteen parties, you should live so long!

*BRIGHTON BEACH: the Jewish Riviera.

SHMOOZING SAUCE BRUN*

2 cups vegetable stock
Salt & pepper, for a real flavor
1 teaspoon MSG
1 bouquet garni (2 sprigs parsley,
  ½ small bay leaf & a pinch
  thyme all tied in a little piece
  cloth)

4 tablespoons *parve* oleo
5 tablespoons flour

First, in a saucepan you'll simmer the stock with the salt, pepper, MSG, and the bouquet garni for maybe 20 minutes. Meantime, in another pan you'll melt the oleo and stir in the flour. Keep stirring until the flour turns into a nice nutty brown—believe me, this is the nicest kind of brown. Take out from the stock the *shmatah* of bouquet garni and pour the stock slowly into the browned flour. You'll be sure to keep stirring, you shouldn't get lumpy. Let the sauce boil till it's thick, then boil 3 minutes more—all the time you're stirring. This is a good sauce to know about. If you add sautéed mushrooms, you'll have a delicious MUSHROOM SAUCE. When you add a little dry red wine, you'll have—what else!—WINE SAUCE. By adding several teaspoons of horseradish, you have an unusual HORSERADISH SAUCE and it goes on and on. The French are nice and smart that way. This sauce makes 2 cups and it's very good poured on meat and anything else you feel like pouring on.

*SHMOOZING: the principle factor in the spectacular growth of AT&T.

HAYMISHA HOLLANDAISE SAUCE*

YOU SHOULD NOTE:

(For *fleischig* meals use *parve* oleo instead of butter)

4 large egg yolks
½ lb. melted sweet butter
1 tablespoon cold water

1 tablespoon lemon juice
A little pinch salt
A sprinkle cayenne pepper

Beat very good the egg yolks in the top of a double boiler and make sure the bottom has hot, but not boiling, water. When the yolks are a nice lemon color and thickened, you'll add *very* slowly, drop by drop (there's no reason to hurry) the melted butter and you'll keep stirring. Even if the phone rings, you'll keep stirring. Soon it'll start to thicken a little like mayonnaise. Dribble in the rest of the butter very slowly and remember, you're still stirring. Add next the lemon juice, salt and pepper. Stir it in a little and it's done. Be careful it doesn't get too hot or, believe me, you won't have Hollandaise Sauce, you'll have scrambled eggs which would look pretty silly sitting on top vegetables, fish or even poached eggs.

HAYMISHA: that nice politician who, when he came to your neighborhood, ate *knishes* and kissed the baby.

BAR MITZVAH BÉARNAISE SAUCE*

2 tablespoons tarragon vinegar
¼ cup dry white wine
2 shallots, chopped
3 egg yolks

½ cup melted *parve* oleo
A small dash cayenne pepper
A little salt
½ teaspoon chopped chervil

A little chopped parsley

First, you'll put the vinegar, wine and shallots in a saucepan and let this boil until half of it is cooked away. Now you'll turn off the fire and put the wine and vinegar mixture aside and start working with a double boiler that has hot, but not boiling, water in the bottom. In this you'll beat good the egg yolks until they're thickened. Then add the melted oleo *very* slowly and you'll stir all the time, until the sauce is nice and thick and the oleo is all poured in. Mix in the wine and vinegar mixture, the pepper, salt, chervil and parsley, and you have now a sauce that's wonderful to serve on steaks and chops. Some people don't think you should put anything on steaks; but, believe me, some of the steaks some people have the nerve to serve should be rescued with a good sauce. BÉARNAISE SAUCE is delicious on all kinds steaks—good and bad.

*BAR MITZVAH: separates the men from the boys.

MEATS

FILET MINYAN WITH MUSHROOM SAUCE*

YOU'LL NEED FIRST:

4 nice thick rib steaks

Take the rib steaks and cut out from the middle of each one the round meaty part. The bones and other things you'll give to the dog or you'll save for a nice soup. Broil these steaks to however you like them. While you're broiling,

YOU'LL FIX NOW THE MUSHROOM SAUCE:

3 tablespoons *parve* oleo	½ cup dry red wine
3 tablespoons flour	A little salt & pepper
1 cup beef broth	1½ cups sliced mushrooms

Cook the flour in 2 tablespoons of oleo, until it's nice and brown. Then you can slowly pour in the beef broth, all the time stirring. Now you'll add the wine, salt and pepper. Let this whole thing simmer uncovered for 15 minutes. Sauté the mushrooms in the rest of the oleo for a few minutes, they should be soft. Mix this in good with the sauce, keep it warm and when the steaks are done, you'll pour over each steak and they're ready to serve 4 Kosher gourmets, they should live to be 120 and still have a hearty appetite.

*MINYAN: when this is needed, no boy over 13 is safe in front of a *shul*.

33

3-4 lbs. lean roast	Salt & black pepper, to taste
2 tablespoons oil	Cayenne pepper, to taste
1½ cups rich beef stock	2 ozs. sherry
2 large onions, quartered	2 cups water
1 bay leaf	2 packages unflavored Kosher
A pinch thyme	gelatin
2 cloves garlic, sliced	

Rub the meat nice with salt and pepper and then brown it in a little oil in a big pot. Then add the beef stock to the pot along with the onions, bay leaf, thyme, garlic, salt, black pepper and cayenne pepper. Now you'll take it easy for about 3 hours while the meat simmers till it's nice and tender. Every now and then, you can stroll into the kitchen and give a little stir to be sure there's still liquid in the pot. You don't have to, but there's something wrong with you if that smell of roast doesn't call you in. When the meat's done, you'll take it from the pot and strain the stock. Now put the stock back into the pot, add the sherry, 2 cups water and boil. From the fire you'll remove. Now add the gelatin (which you just made soft in a little water) and be sure to skim off the fat from the stock. Take a mold and put the meat in it. You decide what kind of mold. It doesn't matter, as long as it's deeper than the meat. Pour over the meat the stock, till the meat is covered. You might skim a little more. Then put the mold in the refrigerator and leave overnight. When it's set, you'll dip the mold in hot water for a few seconds, then turn it upside down on a platter, and so! Decorate here and there with some parsley sprigs, tomato wedges, green pepper rings, curly carrot slices, etc.

   This kind of cold dish you see maybe at weddings and *Bar Mitzvahs* . . . so the family will call you a regular chef when they see this on the table. But then, too, they might say, "So what are we having hot tonight?" Serves about 6 complainers.

OYS GEHMAHTET: how Debbie felt after picketing all day at the Jordan Pavilion at the World's Fair.

BOEUF BOURGUIGNON
DE ROTHSCHILD*

2½ lbs. nice lean beef, cubed
Flour to dust
Salt & pepper, it should have
  a taste
5 tablespoons *parve* oleo
1 large chopped onion
2 cloves garlic, chopped fine

1 chopped carrot
3½ cups dry red wine
1 tablespoon parsley, chopped
1 bay leaf
A good pinch thyme
½ lb. sliced mushrooms
10 small onions

Dust very good the beef with the flour, salt and pepper. Melt 3 tablespoons oleo in a big casserole pot and then throw in the floured meat chunks and brown them a golden color on all sides. While you're browning, you can also throw in the chopped onions, garlic and carrot and push them around a little. When everything is browned nice, pour off the extra fat —be careful you don't pour out your ingredients, too. Next you'll pour in the wine and add the parsley, bay leaf and thyme. Put on the cover and cook in a 350° oven for about 1½ hours. Before you get too comfortable in some other room, you'll sauté first the mushrooms in 1 tablespoon oleo and when that's done, take out from the pan the mushrooms and put aside. Now in the same pan you'll melt the last tablespoon oleo and brown good the small onions whole. Put the onions with the mushrooms and, if your kitchen's not too ventilated, go watch television. After the 1½ hours in the oven, throw in the mushrooms and small onions in the casserole pot and cook covered for another 30 minutes. When it's all done, you should have enough Boeuf for about 6 people who, if they'll call this "stew," you have permission to throw this book at them.

*DE ROTHSCHILD: the nice Jewish family everyone was so friendly with when they moved to town.

FLEMISH CARBONNADES A VOTRE SANTÉ*

2 lbs. chuck cut into 1 inch squares	1–12 oz. can beer
⅓ cup flour	2 teaspoons MSG
4 tablespoons oil	1 tablespoon parsley
3 nice onions, sliced	1 bay leaf
2 tablespoons tomato paste	½ teaspoon thyme
	A few pinches salt & pepper

Dust nice the meat with the flour. Now put the oil into a big pot and cook a little the onions. When they're done, take them out from the oil and put in the pieces meat so they should brown. Now put back into the pot the onions and then the rest of the stuff. Put on the pot the cover, and cook the whole thing on a low fire for 2 hours or, if the butcher sold you tough meat, until it's tender. Don't worry about the beer. For this you don't have to "acquire maybe a taste." It's hidden nice and the whole dish will give 4 to 6 people a hearty appetite.

* À VOTRE SANTÉ: the difference between a continental and a drunk.

36

VEAL CUTLETS CHERCHEZ LA
FEMME WITH CHIVES*

1½ lbs. veal cutlets	1½ cups beef or vegetable stock
⅓ cup flour	1 tablespoon flour
A few pinches salt & pepper	½ teaspoon thyme
4 tablespoons *parve* oleo	2 tablespoons sherry
1 tablespoon chopped chives	

Pound good the cutlets so they're nice and thin. Mix up the salt and pepper with the ⅓ cup flour and dust with this the cutlets. Now put the oleo into a nice size skillet and brown on both sides the cutlets. When they're good and brown, take them out from the pan and put in the stock and 1 tablespoon flour. Now you'll stir good so there shouldn't be lumps. Throw in next the thyme and sherry and scrape from the pan all the little bits of brown stuff. Put the cutlets back in the pan. Put on the cover and you'll simmer for 20 minutes. The last 2 minutes you can throw in the chives. When it's ready, on a dish you'll put the veal and pour on top the sauce. Now it's ready to serve 4 *haymisha* people. If they're on salt-free diets, leave out the pinches salt and you'll still enjoy.

* *CHERCHEZ LA FEMME*: the family plea to Howie who is 25 and still single!

37

PASKUDNIK POT AU FEU*

3½ lbs. beef with the bone (for this is good *flanken*)

2½ quarts water

1 tablespoon salt

1 bouquet garni (bay leaf, pinch thyme, some pepper-corns, sprigs parsley, 1 or 2 cloves—all tied up in a cheesecloth *shmatah*)

2 chopped onions

3 carrots, quartered

1 parsnip, quartered

1 tomato, quartered

2 stalks celery

6 potatoes

The meat you'll put, along with the water, salt, and bouquet garni into a big pot. Bring it to a boil and you'll keep skimming that grey foamy stuff that keeps rising to the top. When the grey stuff doesn't rise anymore, throw in the chopped onions, the carrots, parsnip, tomato and the celery. Put on the cover and let it simmer for 4 hours. At the end of the 4 hours (if you took a nap, you'll be sure to set the alarm) put in the potatoes and let the whole thing simmer for another 45 minutes. To serve this, take from the pot the meat, put in the middle of a nice platter, and around it you'll put the large pieces of the cooked vegetables. From the broth you should skim the fat and serve as a nice soup. Or you can save it for nice stock for other recipes. (For this you'll strain.) The meat should serve at least 5 people. You'll find the meat is very good like it is and even better with:

HORSERADISH SAUCE FOR FANCY FLANKEN

1 tablespoon *parve* oleo

1½ tablespoons flour

1 cup vegetable or beef broth

Salt & pepper to taste

1 tablespoon prepared horseradish

Melt the oleo and dissolve in it the flour. Then pour in nice and slow the broth and let cook for 15 minutes. Put in the salt, pepper and horseradish. Keep heating on a low fire. Put it to the table so if the folks want horseradish on their beef, they'll have.

*PASKUDNIK: the kid who told the neighbors all about his mother's operation.

FOWL

CHICKEN SAUTÉ B'NAI B'RITH*

1–3 lb. chicken, cut up	2 tablespoons rich chicken broth
3 tablespoons *parve* oleo	1 teaspoon lemon juice
¾ cup dry white wine	1 tablespoon curaçao

A little salt

Brown nice the chicken in the oleo and then the wine you'll pour in. Put on the cover and let it cook over a low fire, oh, about 40 minutes, it should be tender. Then you can take it out from the pan and keep it warm. Pour in the pan, the broth, lemon juice, curaçao and the salt. Let this cook for a couple minutes and then over the pieces chicken you'll pour. This makes enough for 3 or 4 people and it's a very popular dish at B'nai B'rith banquets in Aix-en-Provence.

*B'NAI B'RITH: the Jewish answer to the Knights of Columbus.

SHICKER CHICKEN KIEV*

3 large chicken breasts	1 clove garlic, mashed nice
1 tablespoon *parve* margerine, for sautéeing	2 tablespoons chopped parsley
	Salt & pepper to taste
6 mushrooms, chopped very fine	1 tablespoon vodka
½ lb. *parve* margerine, soft	2 eggs
	Bread crumbs, very fine

Take from the chicken breasts the bones with a very sharp knife (and watch you don't leave it around where the kids'll play with it) and separate each breast in 2 halves. Put each half between wax paper and make it flat by pounding a little. Meantime you'll sauté the chopped mushrooms in about 1 tablespoon *parve* margerine. Now cream together the ½ lb. *parve* margerine, garlic, parsley and mushrooms. Chill in refrigerator, then shape it into 6 rolls about 3 inches long and 1 inch wide. Again in the refrigerator you'll put them. Now season those flat chicken breasts with salt and pepper. Place 1 cooled margerine roll on each chicken breast and roll the meat around the roll. Fold in nice the ends so the margerine roll is all inside. If you don't do this, all the margerine leaks out and there goes the Kiev in the chicken! Put toothpicks in the breasts to hold together. Now with the vodka, beat the eggs and roll the chicken in bread crumbs . . . then in the eggs . . . then in the bread crumbs again. Sauté this in plenty *parve* margerine, but not too hot, until the rolls are golden. Drain on a paper towel and put in a hot oven 400° about 5 minutes till the chicken is tender. This serves 3 people and it's so delicious you won't believe it. But with all that margerine it would be a sin to serve dessert. If your company brought some sweet stuff, you can pretend you forgot about it. Serve a little brandy and maybe they'll forget.

*SHICKER: Dean Martin at a Jewish wedding.

41

PUSHKEH POULET CHASSEUR*

2½-3 lbs. chicken, quartered	½ teaspoon chervil
2 tablespoons *parve* oleo	½ teaspoon parsley, chopped
2 shallots, minced	1 can tomatoes
1 cup mushrooms	½ cup dry white wine
1 tablespoon flour	3 or 4 slices bread, fried in
1 teaspoon salt	*parve* oleo
Dash pepper	

Season the pieces chicken so they'll have a good taste. Brown them in oleo on both sides. When that's done, remove them from the skillet and in the leftover oleo you can sauté the shallots and mushrooms. You can add a little oleo if there's nòne left in the pan, because now you have to sprinkle in the flour and stir till it's mixed up with any oleo left in the pan. Add the seasonings, tomatoes and wine and bring to a boil. For about 5 minutes you'll keep cooking. Now, make lower the heat and put the chicken in the sauce. Cover whatever you're cooking in and cook slowly for about 45 minutes or until the chicken is tender and looks good enough to eat. Garnish the chicken with small squares of bread you fried a healthy tan in the oleo. This chicken will have a delicious sauce you shouldn't waste. Maybe you'll make rice or potatoes or maybe you'll serve more bread on the side. Whatever you do is your business and it should make happy 4 or 5 people.

*PUSHKEH: the Jewish Chase Manhattan.

POULET DE LA GOYISHA PUHNIM*

3-4 lbs. quartered chicken
2 cups uncooked rice
2 onions
2 cloves garlic, minced
2 carrots, cooked

1 can peas
2 teaspoons salt
Dash pepper
½ lb. mushrooms
2 cups dry red wine

4 tablespoons *parve* oleo

Sauté the chicken in the oleo until it's a lovely golden. Then you'll take it out from what you're sautéing in and put in a good size casserole pot. Put the rice in the same frying pan and stir till it, too, is a healthy golden brown. Add the onions and garlic and sauté this nice mixture for about 10 or 15 minutes, or until the onion is soft. The frying pan had better be a good size, because now you're adding carrots, peas, salt, pepper, mushrooms and wine. Give a little stir now and then and bring the wine to a boil. Now put the whole thing in the casserole pot with the chicken. Bake it in a moderate oven—say, 350° for about 1 hour, or until the drumsticks are done. Raw chicken, nobody needs. Serve this with a big beautiful salad, a nice glass Kosher wine, it should be dry—and maybe crusty French bread. This will serve 5 to 6 people who'll need extra napkins if they pick up the chicken. And if you pick up, they'll pick up.

GOYISHA PUHNIM: what all beautiful Jewish babies have.

43

ALTE COQ AU VIN*

1 lb. mushrooms, sliced	¼ cup flour
10 small white onions, whole	1 tablespoon parsley
3 shallots, chopped	1 bay leaf
1 clove garlic, chopped	A little salt & pepper
1 medium carrot, chopped	1½ cups dry red wine
4 tablespoons oil	2 teaspoons cornstarch mixed
1-3 lb. chicken, cut in pieces	in 2 teaspoons water

Brown first the mushrooms, onions, shallots, garlic and carrot in half of the oil. Then you can take out from the pan. Now dredge good the chicken in the flour and throw in the rest of the oil into the pan. Brown the chicken in this all over. Put back the vegetables and add the parsley, bay leaf, salt, pepper, and wine. Cover the pan and you'll cook for 1 hour on a very low flame. Just before it's ready, mix in the cornstarch mixture and let it cook for another 2 or 3 minutes. This will make the sauce just thick enough so it should stick to the rice you can serve it with. It makes enough for 4 people and a sauce you'll take pleasure dunking in the next day.

*ALTE: when she walks into the room on *Shabbos,* all the smokers develop cupped hands.

44

CHICKEN LIVERS DE MA
TANTE ROSE*

1 lb. chicken livers	1½ tablespoons flour
3 tablespoons *parve* oleo	½ cup rich beef stock
½ lb. sliced mushrooms	½ cup dry red wine

A little salt & pepper

Salt and broil the livers a little bit on each side, so they should be Kosher. Rinse off from them the salt and in the melted oleo, you'll sauté the livers for about 2 minutes. Put in next the mushrooms and flour and for another 3 minutes you'll sauté and stir so the flour gets nice and brown. Now pour in the rich beef stock and wine and sprinkle in a little salt and pepper so your food should have a nice flavor. Put a cover on the pan and you'll simmer everything together for about 15 minutes. If you serve this on rice, the rice will soak up all that good gravy. This is a healthy dish with lots of nourishment; and if you tell the kids there's wine cooked in, they'll be glad to eat the livers. Serves 3 or 4 iron-starved kids.

* *MA TANTE ROSE:* when you were a kid, she's the one who always said, "You're too pale! Your mother should give you some iron!"

DUCK EN GELÉE À LA GUILLOTINE*

1 4-5 lb. duckling	1 envelope Kosher gelatin, unflavored
2 carrots, skinny	
1 onion	1 egg shell, crumpled up
1 tablespoon parsley	1 teaspoon salt
1 bay leaf	¼ teaspoon white pepper
1 cup dry red wine	½ cup pitted black olives
1 egg white	1 egg, hard-boiled

Simmer good the duck together with the carrots and onion in about a quart of water. Do this in a covered pot for an hour and a half so it'll be tender, the duck. When it's ready, take the duck out from the broth and remove first the skin. This you'll save. Next you'll remove the meat from the bones. This you'll also save. Then you'll skim the broth and *save the fat*. Now put the bones back into the broth and put in also the parsley, bay leaf and red wine. Let this cook on the back of the stove without a cover until it steams down to 2 cups. While you're steaming, you can also fry. Cut up the skin into small pieces and fry it in some of the fat you skimmed a few minutes ago. Do this until they're brown and crisp like a potato chip. Then you can drain and put them aside. And don't nibble! Now stir up the egg white and a crumpled egg shell and throw this mess into the broth. Let it simmer for a few minutes and you'll see how the broth clears. Next you can strain this whole thing through a clean cloth. Mix up the gelatin in a little water and heat it until it melts good. Then throw it into the broth and mix it in. Also mix in the salt and pepper. Now you'll pour enough of this liquid into an 11" x 5" x 3" loaf pan so the bottom gets covered. Put the pan into the refrigerator for a few minutes to set. Then put in a layer duck slices, a layer crisp skin, a layer olives, a layer sliced hard-boiled egg, the 2 whole skinny carrots from before, and another layer duck meat. Pour over this the rest of the liquid and put on top a piece wood for a weight to press it nice. Now the whole thing you should put into the refrigerator and let it chill overnight. To serve, you'll dip the pan into hot water for a few minutes and then turn it upside down on a serving platter. It'll plop right out. Slice it up into slices with a VERY sharp knife and be very careful it shouldn't fall apart. Now it's ready to serve for a cold lunch that'll be so exciting, everybody will be jealous. Serves 5 or 6 hungry, jealous people.

*GUILLOTINE: a dangerous weapon in the hands of the wrong mohel.

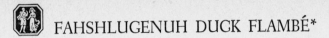

FAHSHLUGENUH DUCK FLAMBÉ*

1-5 lb. duck   ½ teaspoon salt
 3 cups water

FOR THE ORANGE SAUCE, YOU'LL NEED:

1 tablespoon sugar   2 teaspoons cornstarch
1 tablespoon vinegar   ¾ cup orange juice

4 tablespoons brandy

In a covered pot you'll cook good the duck in the salted water for 1 hour. This gets rid of all that extra fat so you should have a healthy gall bladder. Now put the duck into a 425° oven for 45 minutes to finish cooking it to a nice color brown. While you're in the oven, you can skim from the broth the fat. Put aside 1 cup of this broth for the sauce and put the rest into the refrigerator for some other day. Take 1 tablespoon sugar and the vinegar and heat them together in a small pot until the color changes to a dark brown. While you're doing this you can also put into another pot 1 cup of the broth and the cornstarch dissolved in a little water. Heat this and stir it up good until it gets thickened. Then you can throw in the orange juice and the browned caramelized sugar. If it needs, you can throw in a little more sugar. Cook this on a low fire for 5 minutes. When it's almost done, comes the best part. Pour in 2 tablespoons brandy! Ooh, is this going to be a sauce! When the duck is done, into serving pieces you'll cut. Just before you're ready to serve, pour over it the rest of the brandy, a little warmed up, and set it on fire. Serve this with the sauce on the side, so everyone can take what they want. This is enough for 4 people who better eat fast before the Fire Department comes.

*FAHSHLUGENUH: the "helpful" neighbor who gave you a cutting of ivy for the garden and it turned out to be the itchy kind·

FISH

TROUT AMANDINE QVETCH
DE MAMAN*

2 lbs. of trout filets	½ cup slivered almonds
1 egg, beaten	2 tablespoons lemon juice
¼ cup milk	1 teaspoon Worcestershire Sauce
Flour to dredge	1 tablespoon chopped parsley
½ cup butter	Salt & pepper, you'll be generous

Season good the trout with the salt and pepper. Beat up the egg together with the milk and dip in it each piece trout. Then you'll dredge each piece in the flour. ("Dredge" for new brides means to cover the trout with the flour, or you can call your mother-in-law and ask her. She'll be thrilled.) Melt the butter in a frying pan and sauté on both sides the trout until it's nice and brown. Now you'll put it on a warm platter. Put in the frying pan with the leftover butter the almonds, and you'll brown them a little. Add then the lemon juice, Worcestershire Sauce and parsley and warm everything together. Pour this over the trout and it'll make 3 or 4 nice servings. This is a good way to get the kids to eat fish . . . they'll love chewing on those tasty almonds. If you're a new bride, you should ignore that last sentence. If it applies to you anyway, for shame!

*QVETCH DE MAMAN: "I only hope when you have a daughter she talks to you the same way!"

50

FAHPITZT FILET OF SOLE
MEUNIÈRE

6 filets of sole	¼ cup vegetable oil
1 teaspoon salt	4 tablespoons butter
A good pinch pepper	A little lemon juice
¼ cup flour	A little chopped parsley

Wash very good the filets and pat them dry with a paper towel. Mix together the salt, pepper and flour and dust the filets all over. Heat very hot the oil in a frying pan (be sure it's big enough for all the filets) and cook on both sides the fish until they're a lovely golden color, you should be proud! Take them out, drain them to remove the extra oil and put on a warm serving plate. (How you'll get it warm is your problem.) Throw away the oil that's in the frying pan. (If you pour it down the sink, be sure to run the hot water at the same time.) Now, you'll put the butter in the frying pan and let it get brown. Pour the browned butter over the filets, sprinkle on a little lemon juice and parsley and it's a dish fit for a King. Serves 4 to 5 Kings, depending on the size of the filets and the size of the Kings.

*FAHPITZT: describes the "ladies" of Place Pigalle who are the self appointed Welcome Wagon of Paris.

51

COQUILLE DE MON FRÈRE JACQUES*

3 cups cubed halibut	1 tablespoon butter
1 cup dry white wine	3 tablespoons water
1 cup water	2 tablespoons lemon juice
A pinch thyme	⅛ teaspoon pepper
A couple sprigs parsley	2 tablespoons flour
A small bay leaf	1 teaspoon salt
1 celery stalk	2 egg yolks
½ lb. chopped mushrooms	3 tablespoons heavy cream
½ cup chopped scallions	2 tablespoons Parmesan cheese,
1 tablespoon chopped parsley	grated

Enough butter so you can dot

Put the halibut cubes in with the wine, 1 cup water, thyme, the sprigs parsley, bay leaf and the celery in your favorite big pot. Bring it to a boil till it sounds like it might explode, and then you'll lower the fire and cook for another 10 minutes. Take out from this the fish. So you shouldn't burn yourself, use a tablespoon with slots if you have. Put the fish aside and strain the stock and put it back into the nice pot. Throw away

52

the strained stuff, you won't need it anymore. Now boil the stock again until you have only about a cup and a half left. If you're familiar with your own pot, you should know where a cup and a half will be on it. If it's not exact, nobody'll be hurt. Meantime, in another pot, maybe a saucepan, you'll put the mushrooms, scallions, chopped parsley, butter, 3 tablespoons water, lemon juice and pepper. Cover it and cook it on a low fire for 10 minutes. Now you'll stir in the flour and salt and very slowly you'll pour in the cup and a half stock you cooked. Cook it a couple minutes, but don't stop stirring. Turn off now the fire so everything will cool a little bit. In a bowl, beat up the egg yolks with the cream and then slowly pour in the mushroom mish-mash you were cooking in the saucepan. While you're pouring, you should keep stirring. Those pieces halibut that have been standing by you can put in now. Divide this mixture into 6 ovenproof individual serving dishes. Sprinkle on the top the Parmesan cheese, and here and there you'll make a dot with the butter. Stick these 6 dishes under the broiler so they can brown on top, serve and sit back and wait for the compliments. If you don't get any, then you didn't follow the recipe.

* MON FRÈRE JACQUES: my rotten brother Jack who married my old girlfriend and now she's my sister-in-law!

KING SOLOMON'S SALMON
MAYONNAISE*

FIRST, YOU'LL MAKE TAKEH A MAYONNAISE:

2 egg yolks	2 tablespoons tarragon vinegar
1 cup salad oil	1 tablespoon parsley, chopped
½ teaspoon salt	1 clove garlic, minced
¼ teaspoon pepper	½ teaspoon dry mustard

It's sometimes easier if you start with the yolks and oil at room temperature, but it's not absolutely a must. Put the yolks into a mixing bowl, and add salt, and pepper and you'll stir and stir. (In this recipe you never stop with the stirring.) Pour in the oil *very* slowly, drop by drop. If you don't, you'll get one big mess! Keep stirring, keep adding oil, stirring, pouring, until the oil is all poured in and the sauce is thick. Now you'll add vinegar, parsley, garlic, and mustard and stir it all to mix nice.

If the sauce separates, you shouldn't get upset. Don't throw the whole thing out. Just put 1 fresh egg yolk in another bowl and little by little, add the old separated mixture.

If you think you'll keep the mayonnaise a few days, add 1 tablespoon boiling water after it's mixed.

This mayonnaise is not like the store-bought stuff. And if

you don't have the patience to make this kind to serve with your salmon, then close the book and cook TV dinners. And don't be surprised if you'll get hurt looks from that lovely family of yours.

Makes about 2 cups for happy families.

NOW, FOR THE SALMON:

3-7 oz. cans salmon
Shredded lettuce

You'll garnish attractive the bottom of a salad bowl with seasoned shredded lettuce. Smash up the salmon, you'll make sure to remove the skins and bones carefully. Put the salmon on top of the lettuce, spread lots of that tasty mayonnaise on top the salmon and decorate with capers, anchovies, radishes, hardboiled egg slices—anything you think makes nice decoration. The mayonnaise that's left over is wonderful as a sandwich spread. This dish is very nice to eat on *Shabbos* and is a nice change from cold cuts. Serves 4 to 6 people who don't mind smelling from garlic.

KING SOLOMON: the first marriage counsellor in Jerusalem; had 300 wives and was considered a real *mayvin.*

BEI MIR BIST DU SHÖN
BOUILLABAISE*

4 lbs. various *Kosher* fish filets cut in 2-inch pieces	4 minced up cloves garlic
A few fish heads and bones	3 tablespoons oil
A good pinch thyme	2 tablespoons flour
1 tablespoon lemon juice	2 cups tomato sauce
3 bay leaves	2 teaspoons powdered allspice
A few sprigs parsley	Enough salt for a taste
1½ quarts water	A few sprinkles cayenne pepper
2 nice size onions, chopped fine	A good pinch saffron
	½ cup dry white wine

Put the fish heads and the bones together with the thyme, lemon juice, bay leaves and parsley into the pot water. Let it boil good for about 10 minutes without a cover. Don't get worried if some of it disappears . . . it's supposed to. While you're boiling you'll sauté until it's nice and soft, the onions and garlic in the oil. Throw in the flour, it should get nice and

56

brown (this by the French is called a "roux"). By now everything that was boiling should be boiled, so you'll strain the liquid very carefully and throw the other stuff away. Who needs old fish heads and bones and cooked-out spices? Now be sure the liquid is in a big pot . . . and to this you'll add the sautéed onions and garlic and the "roux." Throw in the tomato sauce, allspice, salt, pepper, saffron and the wine. Give a nice stir, and boil everything uncovered for 5 minutes. Put in gently the pieces fish (up to now you've been throwing) . . . put on the cover and let it boil not too fast for 15 minutes.

When you're ready to serve, put a slice or two of toast or thick French bread or even a small mound of cooked rice into each big soup bowl. Put a couple pieces fish in each bowl and then spoon in lots of the soup, which by now should be a nice burnt orange color . . . unless maybe the lighting in my kitchen is different from yours. This is a one-dish meal, you should serve salad with it, and it serves about 5 fish eaters. The aroma from this dish cooking will delight your family, friends and neighborhood cats.

BEI MIR BIST DU SHÖN: I didn't see anything wrong with your *old* nose.

FLOUNDER A LA MOISHE PIPPIK*

FOR THE MOISHE PIPPIK SAUCE, YOU'LL NEED:

1 medium onion, chopped   ½ cup dry red wine
1 tablespoon butter   2 teaspoons flour
¾ cup drained canned   2 tablespoons chopped parsley
   tomatoes, chopped up   A pinch salt
          A good pinch pepper, live it up!

First you'll make the sauce so it can simmer while the fish, it cooks. Sauté the onion in the butter until it's soft. Put the onions in a saucepan together with the tomatoes, wine, flour, parsley, salt and pepper and let it simmer for about 15 minutes, it should get thick. Every now and then you'll give a stir.

PREPARE NOW THE FLOUNDER:

6 flounder filets   2 eggs, beaten up
Salt & pepper for flavoring   ½ cup flour
½ cup milk   1 cup bread crumbs
          1 cup oil

Season the fish very good with salt and pepper. Mix the milk with the egg and dip each filet into the flour, then the egg-mixture, then the bread crumbs. Be very generous with the bread crumbs. Heat the oil in a good size frying pan and fry each filet until it's golden brown on both sides.

When the fish are done, you'll drain them on paper towels or maybe brown paper if you have. On separate plates, you can put a bed of sauce, then the filets go on top the sauce to serve 4 to 6 people. With this meal you should serve a glass wine and you should propose a toast to the man responsible for this dish . . . Count Moishe Pippik!

MOISHE PIPPIK: the famous swashbuckler known to millions as the Count of Monte Cristo.

VEGETABLES

GREEN PEAS TATTELUH
AU TARRAGON*

1 can young spring peas	½ teaspoon MSG
¼ teaspoon dry tarragon	2 teaspoons *parve* oleo
Salt & pepper to taste	2 teaspoons flour

When you open the can peas, pour off half the liquid . . . not all, because you'll make good use of what's left. Now, the peas and the liquid you didn't throw away you'll throw into a saucepan along with the tarragon, salt, pepper and MSG. Cook everything on a low fire until it's nice and heated up. While this is heating, you'll make a *beurre manié*, which don't let the fancy name scare you. The oleo and flour you should knead together so it makes a smooth round ball. Then after you went to all that trouble to make it into one ball, you'll break it up into lots of little pea-size balls. When the peas are hot enough to serve, drop in the little balls of *beurre manié* and stir until they dissolve and the pea juice thickens. This makes, for 5 to 6 people, the most delicious peas you ever had. From this you'll never get thin, but you'll be a happy "heavy."

*TATTELUH: a term of endearment given to little boys before they're old enough to do anything about it.

GREEN PEAS À LA PLACE
DE LA CONCORD*

2 cups shelled peas	A pinch salt
10 leaves of lettuce, shredded	4 tablespoons butter
8 small white onions	A sprig parsley
A pinch basil	¼ cup water

2 teaspoons flour

In a saucepan you'll dump the peas, the lettuce, the onions, the basil, salt, 3 tablespoons butter, parsley and water. Then you'll put on the cover and cook for about 20 minutes until they're tender. While you're cooking you can make a *beurre manié* with the tablespoon of butter that's left and the flour. (This you'll do by kneading together the flour and butter until they're nice and soft.) When the peas are done, you'll break the *beurre manié* into small bits and sprinkle them around on the peas. Give the pan a couple good shakes back and forth so the *beurre manié* can dissolve and make the pea juice nice and thick. And that's all there is to it. You can always use canned peas or frozen peas. But it brings back a lot of memories when you sit and shell peas . . . and it's fun for the kids to do when they're home from school. If you're eating *fleischig* you'll use *parve* oleo instead of butter, it'll be just as good. Serves 5 pea lovers.

*CONCORD: the Jewish Pentagon in the Catskills.

EPPES EGGPLANT AUX
FINES HERBES*

1 medium eggplant	2 chopped shallots
¼ cup *parve* oleo	1 tablespoon chopped parsley
1 chopped onion	1 tablespoon chopped chives
2 cloves garlic, chopped	½ teaspoon marjoram

Salt & pepper for tasting

Slice the eggplant into ½ inch slices and into boiling water you should put them for 3 minutes. Meanwhile, sauté in the oleo the onion, garlic, shallots, parsley, chives, marjoram, salt and pepper. Do this until they're nice and soft. Now take out from the water the slices eggplant and drain them. Then you can put them into a greased baking dish. Smear on each piece eggplant a little of the sautéed mish-mash and put them into a 350° oven for 30 minutes. This makes just enough for 3 or 4 people. Or maybe even just 2 people if they really go crazy when they eat eggplant.

*HERB: in French it's the touch that puts the *haute* in *Haute Cuisine;* in Jewish it's a nice name for a fine Jewish boy.

SA DRAITA ASPARAGUS
POLONAISE*

2 lbs. bunch asparagus	4 tablespoons *parve* oleo
1 hard-boiled egg, chopped	A little salt & pepper
¼ cup bread crumbs	1 tablespoon chopped parsley

Clean and trim good the asparagus and then tie the bunch together with a little string. Put it standing up in a deep pot with about 2 inches salted water in the bottom. On this you'll put a cover and let it steam on a low fire for 15 minutes so they should be tender. If they're still not tender, you'll steam a little more. When they're done, untie them and on a plate you'll put them. Sprinkle on the chopped egg. Now put tne bread crumbs in a pan with the oleo, salt and pepper. Stir it up a little and let it brown good. When this is ready you'll pour it on the asparagus. Next the parsley you should sprinkle on and it's ready to serve 6 pianists who'll play rhapsodies for this dish.

*SA DRAITA: he thought *tour de force* was a guided tour of missile bases.

HOK IN DUH KUPP KIDNEY
BEANS AU VIN ROUGE*

2 cups dried red kidney beans	2 tablespoons *parve* oleo
1 bay leaf	1 small onion, grated
A medium pinch thyme	2 mashed garlic cloves
A few sprigs parsley	2 tablespoons flour
1 stalk celery	A healthy pinch salt
1 small envelope vegetable bouillon	A not-so-healthy pinch pepper
	1 cup dry red wine

Soak the beans overnight with enough water so it should cov... The next day you'll simmer the beans in that same water .. but first you'll add the bay leaf, thyme, parsley, celery, and you'll sprinkle in the bouillon. Simmer all this for 2 hours.

Meantime, about 10 minutes before the beans are done, sauté in the oleo the onion and garlic. Add next the flour, salt and pepper and stir it around until it's nice and smooth. Pour in easy the wine and let this whole thing cook with a medium fire while you stir and it thickens.

When the beans are simmered, the beans you'll drain and then throw away the water with all that stuff that cooked in it. Don't make a mistake and throw away the beans. It would be very embarrassing if the neighbors knew.

Pour the wine-mixture on top of the beans and serve in a colorful casserole pot. The *goyem* almost always cook pork fat with kidney beans. This recipe just goes to show you, kidney beans can live very nicely without all that *hahzarye*.

*HOK IN DUH KUPP: what Seymour got when the girl he picked up in Paris turned out to be a boy . . . . .

BROCCOLI YENTUH
TILLEBENDUH*

3 lbs. broccoli
½ cup butter or *parve* oleo
4 tablespoons lemon juice
1 smashed garlic clove

A little pinch marjoram
A good pinch salt
A nice grind of black pepper

Cut off from the broccoli all that heavy, coarse stuff on the ends . . . who needs it! Wash the broccoli good and put it in a pot with a little salted water in the bottom. Don't drown it— you only want it should steam for about 20 minutes or until it's good and tender. Melt the butter or the oleo (it depends what you'll serve the broccoli with) in a little saucepan and then throw in the rest of the stuff. When it's all mixed together you can pour it on the cooked broccoli and serve. The broccoli shouldn't be so cooked it can fall apart . . . but on the other hand, it shouldn't break your teeth either. You can test the ends with a fork now and then. This is a nice vegetable for 6 people, who, if they don't appreciate good food, won't like this dish.

*YENTUH TILLEBENDUH: a concierge who works for free.

STARCHES

POTATOES RISSOLE À LA
SAMSON'S TZURRIS*

4 medium potatoes	Salt & pepper, to taste
4 tablespoons butter	1 tablespoon parsley

Peel carefully the potatoes and with a fruit scooper (if you don't have one, you'll borrow from the lady next door) scoop out into little balls. Put the balls into a pot with salted water enough to cover and boil it for 8 minutes. When it's boiled, drain the potatoes, but make sure all that steam doesn't burn you. Melt 2 tablespoons butter in a large frying pan and brown half the potatoes—all of them won't fit. Take out from the pan the potatoes and put them aside somewhere not far away. Now you can melt 2 more tablespoons butter and brown the rest of the potatoes. Next you'll put all the potatoes together in a nice looking casserole, sprinkle on salt, pepper and parsley, and warm it in a 250° oven. This will make enough for 4 people who might think you got those round potatoes from a can, until you tell them you scooped.

*SAMSON'S TZURRIS: his girlfriend Delilah gave him such a haircut, it went down in history.

POTATO SOUFFLÉ OY VAY!*

2 cups mashed potatoes
¾ cup light cream
A couple pinches salt

A pinch pepper
2 egg yolks
4 egg whites

First of all your mashed potatoes should be warm. (You can use instant potatoes if you're lazy, or the other kind . . . you choose.) Now the cream you'll mix in together very good with the salt, pepper and egg yolks. With a beater you'll beat the egg whites until they're so stiff they're practically saluting. Then you'll fold the whites into the potato mixture. Put the whole thing into a casserole pot you greased first, and bake it in an oven that says 375°, for a half hour. The soufflé you'll find will get nice and brown on top and it'll rise. Serve it right away when it's done and keep talking so your guests shouldn't notice that it settles down a little as it cools. Serves 4 or 5 talking guests.

*OY VAY!: Grandma's shock when the Paris "hotel" she went into to use the lady's room turned out to be the Egyptian Embassy.

MARVIN'S POMMES DE TERRE
À SAVOIR FAIRE*

4 large potatoes, peeled & sliced thin	2 cups milk
1 teaspoon salt	1 tablespoon butter
A few sprinkles black pepper	½ cup heavy cream

¼ cup grated Parmesan cheese

Put the potatoes, salt and pepper together with the milk in a double boiler. Let it cook a half hour, you'll be sure it's covered. Now you'll shmear well a baking dish with 1 tablespoon of butter and put the potato-milk mixture in it. Over this you'll pour the cream, then sprinkle on the Parmesan cheese. Put the whole thing uncovered into a 350° oven for 25 minutes so the top, it gets browned. This dish is very good to help 6 undernourished people get some meat on their bones, or serves 5 people who don't care how much meat they get on their bones.

*MARVIN'S SAVIOR FAIRE: when the newlyweds told him they were expecting, he counted the months on his fingers behind his back.

MITTEN DE RINNIN RICE
AUX CHAMPIGNONS*

2 tablespoons *parve* oleo
1 medium onion, chopped
1 cup sliced mushrooms

1 cup rice
2 cups nice chicken broth
A good pinch salt

Melt first the oleo and in it you'll put the onion and mushrooms and cook until the onions are nice and soft. Next you'll dump in the rice and mix everything all together. While you're mixing, you should also boil the chicken broth and the salt. Then over the rice you'll pour the boiling broth, put on the pot the cover, and cook on a low fire for 20 minutes. If it comes out maybe a little dry, you'll sprinkle on a little more broth. To make this dish good, be sure you have nice rice that isn't all stuck together. If it is, don't tell them where you got the recipe. That kind of business, who needs? Serves 3 to 4 champions.

*MITTEN DE RINNIN: you're on the front row half way through a Broadway play, and Bobby whispers he has to "go" . .

70

DESSERTS

BLINTZ SUZETTE*

This dish, like Gaul, is divided in three parts:

FIRST, THERE'S THE BATTER:

1 cup sifted flour   1 cup milk
A good pinch salt   4 nice fresh eggs, beaten up

Sift together the flour with the salt. Then you can mix up the milk and eggs with it. For this a blender is good. Now take a 6 inch pan and shmear in it a little butter. Pour some batter in the pan and tilt it around a little so it gets spread out nice. If you don't pour too much batter and you tilt good the pan, the cake will be nice and thin. Cook on a low fire until the top gets a little dry. Then it's done. Take it out from the pan and on a cloth or a napkin you'll put it to cool. Keep doing this until you're all used up.

NOW COMES THE FILLING:

1 lb. nice dry cottage cheese   1 tablespoon melted butter
1 beaten egg yolk   3 tablespoons sugar
A pinch salt

Mix good together all this stuff. Now taste it. If you like a little sweeter, put in more sugar. Now you can divide a little of this on each cake. Fold the cake like an envelope (or like a blintz). After this, into a greased pan you'll put them and bake them nice in a 350° oven for 20 minutes.

AND LAST, BUT NOT LEAST, THE SAUCE:

½ cup butter
½ cup powdered sugar
¼ teaspoon dried orange peel

1 teaspoon lemon juice
¼ cup orange juice
¼ cup curaçao

Melt together with the butter, the sugar. Then put in the orange peel, lemon juice, orange juice, and curaçao. Mix it all together nice and some of this you'll pour on each serving blintzes. Then on each serving you'll also pour a little brandy. This you can set on fire and serve right away, you shouldn't burn yourself. You'll have enough to serve 4 people 2 blintzes each, with maybe a blintz or two left over, which you can eat like a sneak in the kitchen while you're doing the dishes. Such a *hahzar!*

* BLINTZ: a crêpe with a superiority complex.

BUBBA AU RHUM*

FOR THE CAKE PART, YOU'LL NEED:

2 cups flour	A pinch salt
1 envelope yeast	1 tablespoon sugar
½ cup warm water	1 tablespoon raisins
4 eggs, beaten	1 tablespoon dry currants
¼ cup butter	1 teaspoon grated lemon rind

Sift first the flour and then dissolve the yeast in the warm water and pour it on the flour, which let's hope is in a bowl. Now add the eggs and with your hands you'll squish around until the dough is like rubber. Next, mix in good the butter. Cover up the bowl of dough with a cloth, it should be clean, and put it in a warm place to rise until it's twice as big. This should take maybe 1½ hours. Now you can punch down the dough and work in the salt, the sugar, raisins, currants, and lemon rind. You'll work out a lot of frustrations when you play with this dough. If you don't have a fancy mold for this (like I don't), you can use even a 12 muffin muffin-tin, it's just as good. Grease very nice the muffin-tin and you'll put the dough in the 12 holes, the same amount in each one. Each hole or mold should be maybe ⅔ full and don't worry if the top doesn't look so smooth . . . it'll smooth by itself. Put the molds or the muffin-tin in that warm place you used before for the bowl of dough and let it rise until all the cakes are about ¼ inch above the top. This should take maybe a half hour. Then put the muffin-tin or molds in a 425° oven, and bake for 15 minutes. When you stick in a toothpick, it should come out clean. When they're done, lift them out from the tin or the molds and put them aside; you're not finished yet.

74

NOW FOR THE BEST PART—THE "RHUM" PART:

2 cups water
1 cup sugar
⅔ cup rum

Together you'll boil the water and sugar until you have a clear syrup. Then mix in the rum. With a skewer you'll poke lots of holes in the çakes and you'll arrange them in a deep dish and pour over them the rum syrup. Your kitchen might smell a little like the Bowery, but with class! Let them sit like this for ½ hour and every now and then you'll give another baste. Then drain them for maybe 15 minutes.

AND, FINALLY, HERE IS A GLAZE TO SCHMALTZ UP THE WHOLE THING:

3 tablespoons apricot preserves
2 tablespoons water

Put the preserves and water together in a saucepan. Heat and stir until it's nice and smooth. Now with a little brush you'll paint the top of each cake to make a nice glaze, put them in the refrigerator and you'll later have a dessert to serve nobody'll believe you made. Serves 12 *bubbas* who'll be very happy to eat a dessert named after them. And it wouldn't be a bad idea you should give them also a copy of this book, they'll have their own recipe.

* *BUBBA AU RHUM:* Grandma after her first nightclub visit!

75

TOUT DE SUITE STRAWBERRIES
AVEC COGNAC*

1 quart of strawberries
½ cup sugar
⅓ cup cognac

6 slices sponge cake, already made

If you don't have a quart to measure the strawberries, you'll find 2 baskets of strawberries make 1 quart. Wash carefully the strawberries and take off from them the green things. Put in a big bowl the cleaned up strawberries and sprinkle on all over the sugar. Put it in the refrigerator for about an hour so they'll be cold. Every now and then you'll stroll in and give a stir and maybe steal a berry. When you're ready to serve, pour over it the cognac. In 6 plates you'll put a slice of sponge cake —you can get the recipe from Jennie Grossinger's book—dish out the berries over the slices cake and pour the extra juice on, too. This is a nice dessert for 6 people, if you didn't steal too many berries when you were chilling.

*TOUT DE SUITE: refers to Shelly's wedding after her summer in the Catskills.

PEARS FOLIES BERGÈRE*

6 fresh pears   1 cup sugar
½ cup dry red wine   1 small stick cinnamon
          1 small piece lemon peel

First you should peel the pears, cut them in half and take out from them the cores. In a saucepan you'll mix together the wine, sugar, cinnamon, and lemon peel. Bring this to a nice, healthy boil and cook a few pear halves at a time until they're soft. (If all 12 halves fit in your pot, you've got some pot!) Now take out from the syrup the cinnamon and lemon peel and cook the liquid until only about half of it is left. Pour this over the pears and put them in the refrigerator, they should be served cold enough to hurt the fillings in the teeth. Serves 6 people whose class had fewer cavities.

* *FOLIES BERGÈRE:* France's answer to the Hadassah Chanukah skit.

TZIMMIS DE FRUITE FLAMBÉ*

2 lbs. of dried fruits (apricots, prunes, raisins)	1 cup water
1 cup orange juice	½ cup rice
2 teaspoons sugar	2 tablespoons curaçao
	½ cup brandy

Wash the fruit carefully and drain it nice, it should be dry. Put it aside for a few minutes, and bring the orange juice, sugar and water to a boil in a pretty casserole pot. Add next the fruit and rice, you'll simmer in the casserole for 20 minutes, and make sure it's covered. When the rice is tender, and stir once in awhile so it doesn't stick, stir in the curaçao and sprinkle on the brandy and bring it to the table. (Now you see why the casserole should be pretty . . . because everybody has to look at it.) Turn off the lights and hurry, before everyone gets scared, and light the brandy. This will light up 6 people.

* *TZIMMIS*: what Murray's wife made when he overtipped the French maid.

POTCHKUH MOUSSE AU CHOCOLAT*

2 1-oz. squares of semi-
  sweet chocolate
½ cup water
1 tablespoon unflavored
  Kosher gelatin
¼ cup cold water

3 egg yolks
2 tablespoons sugar
A pinch salt
1 tablespoon curaçao
1 tablespoon sugar
3 egg whites

Melt the chocolate in the ½ cup water on a low fire. While you're melting, the gelatin you'll soften in the ¼ cup cold water and then mix it into he chocolate. Beat now the egg yolks together with the 2 tablespoons sugar and this, too, you'll pour into the chocolate stuff along with the salt and the curaçao. (Curaçao is used so much in this book, you'd better run out and buy some for the house. Besides it looks good in the kitchen.) Now into a dry clean bowl—and, believe me, it better be dry—dump the egg whites and another pinch salt and with a dry beater, you'll beat like crazy until the egg whites make like little peaks. (So many mousses I had to make to do this recipe! So you don't be smart and try short cuts.) Now add the 1 tablespoon sugar to the beaten egg whites and again you'll beat until it's so stiff, if you put a whole egg on top, it wouldn't sink. (I'm not joking . . . that's how stiff you have to be.) Take a big spoonful of the beaten whites and mix it in with the chocolate mixture. Now put the rest of the beaten whites on top the chocolate mixture and fold in very gently with a spatula. If all the white doesn't mix in too well . . . that's all right, too. Because if you don't fold gently, you might push from the egg whites too much air . . . and then you'll have a mashed mousse. Put the bowl in the refrigerator to chill good for a few hours and then you can serve about 6 people who, let's hope, they didn't bring over their own dessert.

*POTCHKUH: what kids do when they look for the chocolate -with the cherry in the middle.

QUELLE HEURE EST-IL CAFÉ
AU LAIT?*

For this kind coffee you should use a porcelain coffee pot instead of an aluminum pot which will only get black from the water, sooner or later.

Ahead of time, you can make a very strong coffee they call *café noir*, which is no small coincidence, it means black coffee. (Those nice smart Frenchmen think of everything.) You boil some water and first you'll rinse out the basket and the lower half of the coffee pot with a little of the water. Don't ask why —but a real coffee maker *mayvin* does this; so you don't ask questions, just do. Then fill the basket with coffee. Now some people say you should use 1 tablespoon coffee for each tablespoon water . . . but this will give you such a strong coffee, you'll have hair on your chest! So you may have to try a few times and see how strong you like it. In my pot I use 8 tablespoons coffee and 2 cups boiling water. Now slowly, you'll pour over the coffee the boiling water, until it's all used up. When it's all through dripping into the bottom of the pot, you'll put the *café noir* in a jar and refrigerate until you need it, or you can take a little and have a cup coffee right now. You can make all you want, and just heat it up every time you want some. This isn't like the usual coffee you have to have fresh every time.

To make the CAFÉ AU LAIT, which it turns out is a very weak and very tasty French coffee, you heat up the *café noir* (never boil it; just heat it) and put a little in each coffee cup —say, about ⅓ or ½ full. And then you'll pour very hot milk to the top of the cup.

This the French always have after a *milchig* meal. It takes a little more time than the usual type of coffee, but you won't get as nervous.

*QUELLE HEURE EST-IL? this is the longest sermon he's ever made!

INDEX

81